MAKING
MONEY AT HOME

MAKING
MONEY AT HOME

CONSUMERS' ASSOCIATION

Which? Books are commissioned and researched by
Consumers' Association and published by
Which? Ltd,
2 Marylebone Road, London NW1 4DF
Email address: books@which.net

Distributed by The Penguin Group:
Penguin Books Ltd, 27 Wrights Lane, London W8 5TZ

First edition October 1997
Copyright © 1997 Which? Ltd

British Library Cataloguing in Publication Data
A catalogue record for this book is available from the British
Library

ISBN 0 85202 691 9

The text of *Making Money at Home* is based on material in *The
Which? Guide to Earning Money at Home* by Lynn Underwood

For a full list of Which? books, please write to Which? Books,
Castlemead, Gascoyne Way, Hertford X, SG14 1LH
or access our website at http://www.which.net

Cartoons and cover illustration by David Pattison, Cartoon
Partnership
Cover design by Creation Communications
Typeset by Saxon Graphics Ltd, Derby
Printed and bound in Great Britain by Caledonian International
Book Manufacturers, Glasgow

CONTENTS

* in text denotes address at back of book

INTRODUCTION

These are the sorts of people this book is aimed at.

LINDA is a young mother with a baby. She realised that if she worked full-time in a shop she would barely be able to make enough money to pay for childcare, let alone pay the bills. She saw an advertisement in the local paper for homeworkers: the work turned out to be for packing greetings cards. She took the job and has found that in a good week she can make enough to pay a few of the bills. The work is repetitive but not unpleasant; she can do quite a lot in the evenings, and sometimes her husband helps her. The company requested that she should be self-employed and there-fore take care of her own tax and National Insurance. Because of her low earnings she has not yet paid tax.

BARRY is disabled and although he is a qualified teacher he was finding the demands of school life too great. He decided to set up at home as a private tutor. The pupils come to him for their lessons, and most of his work is in the early evenings and at weekends. He also makes extra income by invigilating at examina-tions and marking the papers.

MARION is a middle-aged housewife whose children are in their late teens. Her husband earns a good salary but Marion wanted to have some independence. She decided to take a course in basic computer skills and enjoyed it so much that she graduated to more specialist software courses. A friend put her in touch with a publishing house and now, from home, she typesets book manuscripts on to computer disks which are then passed to the printers. She works about four hours a day.

ERIC took early retirement and decided to develop his hobby into a small money-making enterprise. He now makes wooden toys which he sells at craft fairs; his wife often runs the stalls as she enjoys the friendly atmosphere and the marketing side of the business.

This book aims to give advice to anyone contemplating working from home, whether in a part-time or a full-time capaity. But note that working at home is not suited to everyone, nor to every family situation. It requires self-discipline, self-reliance, organisation and determination. The book does not attempt to go into great detail about every issue relating to business as there are other books devoted to more specifiic issues – see in particular *The Which? Guide to Starting Your Own Business*. But it does highlight the possibilities for the would-be home worker.

Why work from home?

1

The reasons why people choose to work from home are as diverse as the ways they choose to earn their money. For some, the desire to opt out of the rat race, the pressures of daily commuting, the personality clashes in the big company or factory take precedence over the security of a monthly salary cheque.

The advantages

There are many advantages to working from home, depending upon your chosen occupation and your personality.

- You save a considerable amount of money by not travelling to your place of work and, if you are self-employed, by not having to rent or buy other premises.
- If you use part of your own home for work you can claim part of the costs of the mortgage or rent, heating, lighting and telephone. Any alterations or repairs done to the premises which are directly related to improving your working conditions can also be put through your accounts.
- You can work during the hours you would otherwise spend in travelling.

- You can take advantage of certain types of work that can be fitted into your children's day.
- You may want to work unconventional hours. A writer may be able to work any hour of the day or night, whereas a mobile hairdresser may find that her clients want appointments during the daytime or early evening only.
- You can wear whatever you like, you have control over your environment – the temperature, the lighting – and when you take your lunch break.
- You need no longer be a weekend parent.
- You may be able to enlist the help of your family to get tasks completed.
- You can decide just how much work you want to take on. You may simply be trying to generate a little extra money. You may be capable of coping with only a certain amount of concentrated physical or

mental effort. You may just want an occupation to fill in the spare time, or you may be prepared to work every hour available.

The disadvantages

- There could be restrictions that prevent you from using your home as a work base. Before starting, check the details of all leases, deeds, charges and covenants to see whether running a business in your home is prohibited. Similarly, local bylaws may prohibit any occupations which involve a fire risk, noisy machinery or frequent deliveries.
- You may need planning permission if your home-based occupation changes the use of a building: for example, turning your garden into a cattery. Generally, if you are using less than half your house as office space, or your shed as a workshop, you don't have to apply for planning permission. The key to it all is unobtrusiveness. The local authority will be concerned not just over 'change of use' but also whether your business will contribute to noise or air pollution, whether you are planning any structural alterations to your house and whether your activities come under the scrutiny of the department concerned with health and safety.
- Your home contents insurance policy will certainly have to be extended to cover your work materials, records and also outbuildings if you are using them for storage or as workshops. You will need to consider other forms of insurance – public liability, pro-

11

fessional indemnity and some form of private health insurance and pension.

- You need to pay greater attention to home security if your whole livelihood is housed in your home. For instance, you may have high-value, easily portable equipment, and you will almost certainly have to publicise your home address, or at least the telephone number, in some way. Outbuildings are at even greater risk. Seek advice from the local police.
- You may find life at home too distracting.
- If you don't have a family you may hate the solitude.
- Because you can't leave the pressures of work at an office, or expect the family to talk in whispers, resentments may build up. You have to be sure that you have a personality that can adapt to working at home. People who have sedentary home-based jobs need to be self-disciplined yet relaxed, able to work as many hours as needed, then shut work off and give the family some time too.
- Working for yourself can mean insecurity. Will enough money come in to pay next month's bills? Will customers pay on time or will you have to chase them? Can you get the work done on time? Will the demand for your product or service continue?
- Working for someone else can also mean insecurity. Have one or two sources of part-time work on the go at once, so that if one fails you can perhaps increase the hours on another.
- Working for someone else can sometimes mean repetitive, time-consuming and poorly paid work. Do you have the patience to stuff envelopes all day

long? You may have to process thousands of pieces a week to make a living wage.

- There are home-based jobs where the employee has the telephone bill paid but earns commission only on successful conversions into sales. This can mean making hundreds of telephone calls without earning anything at all.
- You may have to pound the pavements. Some people deliver catalogues, directories, local newspapers or leaflets. Others do house-to-house surveys. The work has to be done whatever the weather, and, quite often, during the evenings.
- Collecting money door-to-door for football pools, Christmas clubs or catalogues can be hazardous. Walking the streets at a regular time each week with large amounts of cash is an invitation to muggers.

Preparation is the key to success

Once you have analysed your motives for working from home and weighed up the advantages and disadvantages, you are halfway to preparing yourself for a fruitful and satisfying working life.

If you are contemplating earning money from home, however modestly, work out a business plan to prepare yourself for any direction in which your occupation may take you.

This may seem unnecessary – after all, you are only decorating a few wedding cakes, aren't you? But what happens if one of your wedding cakes is so admired by a professional baker that he offers you a contract to decorate 20 cakes a week for his two shops? Suddenly

13

you are catapulted from a paying hobby into a small business. You hadn't planned on it; you didn't actively market yourself, it just happened. Without preparation you are lost – the effort of meeting the orders leaves you no time to sort out accounts, get some back-up help, get your kitchen up to professional standards and deal with the authorities if necessary.

If you had investigated every possible business scenario before you even started your venture, gathered the information needed for possible expansion and sorted out a fail-safe mechanism should things go wrong, you would have laid the foundations for success or, at the very least, a painless withdrawal from something that did not work out as you had hoped.

What if?

This is the question you should ask yourself in the preparation stage and then discuss the answers with your family, friends, investors or advisers. What if ...

- **No one wants my product or services?** Have you researched the marketplace to gauge demand? Can you adapt in some way to appeal to a different market sector? Can you diversify using the same materials/skills?
- **I can't make enough money from each piece of work to make a profit?** If the market isn't there, can you produce cheaper items that are less labour-intensive and have a higher profit margin? Would you make more money if you offered your skills for only part of the process?

14

- **I get more work than I can handle?** This may be no more than getting to know people in your area with related skills, finding out their availability and letting them know that you may need their help at some point. Before you start up you can decide which people could help you if the orders came thick and fast. There may be someone who is also self-employed in a similar trade to whom you could sub-contract. Many people get caught off-guard when they are suddenly offered a large contract and grab it too quickly without adjusting prices to allow for the employment of extra staff.

- **I become ill?** Again, you need to have back-up mechanisms set in place wherever possible. You also need a private health insurance scheme that will pay you enough money to cover all overheads during your period of sickness and, perhaps, what is known as a 'keyman' policy which can cover you against any business losses incurred by accident or ill-health.

- **My children become ill?** How much money will you lose if you look after them yourself? If you have a deadline to meet, or a new contract that is worth a lot of money to you, perhaps you can have someone to stay for the period of the illness or you can pay a friend to child-sit. If this scenario is discussed with the parties concerned early on you will not have to worry about it.

- **I need more equipment?** If you can, budget at the beginning for future expansion. If you can't put money away you will have to borrow the money to buy equipment outright, or investigate leasing or hire terms. Talk to staff at your bank: you will need to present some sort of business plan and discuss what they may be able to offer you and what they will charge for loans or overdraft facilities. It may work out cheaper to lease equipment than to have a bank loan. But make all the enquiries at the beginning.

- **I need to extend the house?** Talk it over with family, local authority and neighbours long before you ever need to do anything. You can even go through the whole process of drawing up plans and getting planning permission (the permission lasts for five years before it has to be resubmitted). It may also be the case that the local authority would refuse planning permission.

- **Customers won't pay their bills?** You have to be very strict about payment terms, invoicing, and charging interest to late payers. Don't do commissioned work on credit; ask for payments along the way. Find out what your solicitor will charge for sending intimidating letters to bad payers – some solicitors now offer a cheap service for this. Make a resolution that if anyone defaults on a bill more than twice you will no longer work for them.

- **Employers don't pay me?** If an employer defaults, find out why. If it is because of business failure, you will have to get in touch with the Official Receiver and put in your bid for monies owed to you. If it is for some other reason you need the advice of ACAS and perhaps a solicitor. It is best to know all your rights before even seeking home employment.

WHAT CAN YOU DO?

2

You have analysed your motives, needs and personality and decided that earning money at home would suit you perfectly. The question is how to earn it. You may already know exactly what you want to do, but if you do not, look at the options.

Translate an existing job into a home-based one

Many teleworkers have started by asking their employees to let them work from home. This is ideal because you are doing a job which obviously suits you very well in terms of skills and aptitude and you are still an employee, with the attendant financial security.

You may be happy doing your current job but not happy to be an employee. Provided you have done your market research and made the necessary contacts to ensure a healthy supply of work, things should go smoothly. Hairdressers, chiropodists, upholsterers and typists, for example, can all go down this route, offering a visiting service to clients in their own homes or have clients come to them.

Develop new skills by training part-time

This is a popular route to a new career for people who are approaching retirement or for women who are returning to the job market after several years. Many

17

younger people, frustrated in full-time employment that offers no stimulation, have also turned to adult education classes to provide them with new qualifications. An unprecedented number of training schemes, diploma courses and business courses are on offer.

It is possible to acquire certain skills, provided one has a talent for them, in just a few months. Cake-decorating, picture-framing and computer skills are examples.

Sometimes people are already skilled in certain areas but feel that they need the appropriate diplomas to give extra confidence to their customers. In this case it may be possible, by arrangement with the local adult education institute, just to sit the examinations. Areas where it is common for individuals to do this are car mechanics, dressmaking, floristry, beauty therapy, hairdressing and catering.

Develop an interest into a service

Some ventures do not require any particular skills, just a keen interest in the subject, such as looking after children or pets and gardening. Check with your local authority about regulations.

Develop a hobby into a business

It is not unusual to make a hobby pay in some small way. Materials are so expensive that very few people can afford to, say, make picture frames without occasionally offering them for sale so that they can buy new materials. Sometimes skilled hobbyists are started on the self-employment road by donating a piece of work to a charitable sale and being surprised by how swiftly it sells.

Do unskilled work at home for someone else

This may be the only option if you have no skills or hobbies to develop and no time to train for a new career. Many of the people who work at home for an outside employer are doing the type of work generally done in a factory, assembling anything from watch straps to fire extinguishers, making toys or lamp-shades, filling Christmas crackers and so on. A lot of this type of work is done for the clothing industry. Much of the work is repetitive, requires little skill (but lots of attention) and does not lead to the satisfaction of seeing the finished product.

Finding such work and ensuring that you are getting a fair deal is not easy. It has to be approached with some caution and it is best to be aware of possible pit-falls before answering advertisements for unskilled homework (see Chapter 3).

Do skilled work at home for someone else

This is a more promising line because if you have a skill that is in demand you will be paid a reasonable rate by an employer, but work may be more difficult to find and may require some marketing on your part. For example, if you are a skilled knitter but you do not want to work for yourself you may have to approach local shops to see if they would be interested in paying

19

for your garments. Many clothing manufacturers employ homeworkers to sew parts of garments together or to finish or inspect them. Most employers are honest and fair but the textile and clothing industries have had a bad reputation in the past for taking advantage of homeworkers.

Turn your house or land into a money-earner

There are many ways in which you can make your property earn you some money, such as taking in lodgers or converting a room into a tea room, even an art gallery. However, such ventures mean a change of use, permission from the local authority and, if you are going into an endeavour which involves serving food to the public, however modest, the Environmental

Health Department will demand all kinds of changes to your premises to comply with the various regulations.

Making use of land sometimes requires local authority consent. Planting an acre of vegetables does not, but keeping livestock or running a cattery, kennels or caravan or camping site does.

Parts of a very large house or suitably dry outbuildings can be used as storage space for people who, say, want to store furniture while they are abroad. Also (again with the consent of the local authority) outbuildings can be rented out to people as workshops.

Sell goods made by other people

If you enjoy meeting people, can be persuasive, have the courage to test new ground and can handle rejection, perhaps you can come to an arrangement with a friend who produces marketable items but doesn't have the time to sell them. You could agree on a commission on each item sold. Many people make a good living out of being agents for mail-order companies. They earn commission on each item paid for by the customers they get on to their books.

Some publishers now sell straight into homes and schools rather than through bookshops, as the percentage of the cover price taken by the wholesalers and the retail shops is far greater than the commission paid to agents.

Other people sell successfully through 'party' schemes, offering well-known brands of clothing, jewellery, toys and underwear. This involves getting as many customers as possible together at a friend's

21

house for a 'party' and persuading them to place orders. The object is to hold parties in as many different areas as possible so that you tap into many groups.

Network marketing or pyramid selling is another possibility. Most network marketing schemes require the participants to buy the goods or services and then sell them on. Participants also receive bonuses for recruiting other sales staff and take commissions on the recruit's sales. Sometimes payments are demanded by the parent companies for providing training to the sales force. Many people join these schemes because they are impressed by the success stories, but the truth is that only those who are recruited in the early days of such schemes are able to make a lot of money earning commissions from other recruits. Participants who come in at the 'bottom of the pyramid' have very little chance of making big money because the products on sale can support a sales network of only a certain size.

WHAT IS IT THAT WILL ACTUALLY EARN YOU MONEY?

Is it your **skill**? Do you know whether your skill is in demand, whether it has scarcity value, or whether it represents a luxury in today's society?

Think of a skill that is in demand – invisible mending, perhaps. Commuters damage suits which then need to be repaired. The logical place to take them is to the dry cleaners. Every dry cleaner offers invisible mending and this is usually done by homeworkers. So you offer your services to every dry-cleaning shop. If they don't need you now, they may keep you on file for later.

Think of a skill that is rare. There is a lack of watch repairers in towns today, for example. Jewellers employ such craftsmen but, again, they are usually homeworkers. You could offer them your services, but you may think that there are enough people around with watch problems to make it worth your while to advertise locally.

Perhaps you are a management consultant, skilled at assessing a company's problems and coming up with the appropriate solutions. But does the economic climate affect your value? Are you a need, or have you become a luxury?

Perhaps what you are really selling is your **time**? Your skills may be limited, and your most valuable asset is that you can serve those customers who do not have the time to perform certain tasks themselves, such as ironing, lawnmowing, window-cleaning, dog-walking, cooking, typing, and so on.

Then, again, perhaps it is your **effort** that is most valuable? You can do all the heavy or unpleasant jobs that your customers cannot manage – digging, building and repairs, tree-felling, cleaning out drains, chimney-sweeping and so on.

Perhaps your customers come to you for your **ingenuity, analytical skills** and **flair** when they want a problem solved, a new image, a new direction. You may be a graphic artist, a PR specialist, an interior designer or a clothes designer.

23

Or is it your **specialist knowledge** and **skill** that will earn the money? Others benefit from your knowledge in certain areas because you do research for them, you give them health and beauty therapy or you advise them on insurance and pension plans. Perhaps you drive a taxi? You can write articles or give demonstrations on your specialist subject.

You may have **qualifications** which equip you to train others. You are a tutor in your own home to children who need extra tuition; you teach a musical instrument, or you train people to drive cars. Perhaps you help adults to learn to read and write in the privacy of your home or you teach people to speak a language. Cookery and needlework can be taught at home, as many crafts.

Maybe it's your **personality** that earns you money, enabling you to sell effectively, to keep children amused all day, or to look after sick or elderly people. You may have the skills and qualifications to be a hairdresser or chiropodist but very few customers will invite you to their homes if you don't have a warm personality.

Whatever your field, do as much research as possible. Talk to people, read newspapers and magazines. Keep a file of information, articles and comments.

WORKING FOR SOMEONE ELSE AT HOME

A large variety of work is available to homeworkers but the work is often irregular and low-paid. Most companies using homeworkers prefer them to be self-employed because it is cheaper (no overheads for the company) and they do not have as much responsibility for self-employed workers as they would for employees. However, this matter of 'employed' or 'self-employed' is a grey area. The overriding factor seems to be that if the person you work for deducts tax from your pay, you are an employee. Some companies deduct tax from their workers' money but expect them to pay their own National Insurance. The Low Pay Units advises all homeworkers to keep strict records of hours worked, whether the work is regular, whether they have any sort of contract or agreement, what they are paid and whether any deductions are made. This information may be useful later if you need to prove that you were actually an employee in order to claim some sort of compensation.

Working at home as an employee

You may have been offered by your employer the opportunity to do the same job at home. If you are

extremely lucky you will have the same benefits –
employee status, pension scheme, paid holidays, paid
sickness time and so on.

Most homeworkers are self-employed. Some people
prefer that because it enables them to work for several
people at the same time. However, the reality is that
most homeworkers are tied to one 'customer' who
gives them large volumes of time-consuming work that
does not pay a great deal.

Watch out for the piecework rate that actually means
you are working for only pence an hour, because the
company says it takes far less time to produce an item
than is actually possible. There *are* reasonable companies that give decent rates for a job – but you have to
shop around carefully.

Advertisements

Look in the local newspaper or in a trade paper if you have a skill appropriate to a particular industry. Many such advertisements promise high earnings very quickly. These are probably pyramid selling/network marketing schemes – the main giveaway is that you are expected to recruit others as well as sell. It is best not to join any scheme which asks you to purchase goods or stocks or pay for training.

Never send money in advance for anything. A *bona fide* advertisement should supply a telephone number from which you can find out a company name, address and full written details of the work.

If you are interested in a particular homeworking opportunity check the company or scheme with your local Trading Standards Office, which will know whether a scheme is dubious, and your nearest Low Pay Unit/Homeworking Group, which will be able to tell you whether a particular company has been black-listed for any reason. Not all regions have LPUs.

Local or national firms

Contact local companies to see whether they have any homeworking opportunities. If you have any previous relevant work experience, tell them about it, and also whether you have any equipment of your own at home – word-processor, sewing-machine – and what hours you may be able to work. Also tell them about any skills that you have. Running social groups can be as valuable as any work experience.

27

Other routes

Ask your local unions if they know of any opportunities. The JobCentre may also have some homeworking on its books. Your nearest Homeworker Group or Low Pay Unit will certainly know. People with disabilities can contact RADAR* or the Disability Alliance.* Teleworkers can contact the Telecottage Association.* Ask friends and neighbours.

When you find work

You need to ask yourself, or the company offering the work, the following questions before accepting:

- Have you done this type of work before? Is any training given? Does it involve assembling materials and do you have the room to spread the work out? Can you meet the delivery dates? Is your eyesight up to it? What quality of work will you be expected to deliver and how will that quality be measured? Will someone help you to achieve the necessary standard?
- Find out how much work you have to do to make a living wage or how many pieces have to be completed for the company to continue giving you work.
- Is there a co-ordinator to turn to for advice? It is not enough to have contact once a week or less with the person who delivers your work. You need to have access over the telephone to someone who can answer your day-to-day queries.

- You need a manual that explains your equipment so that you can cope with any problems. Some companies have specification manuals because they are producing items of clothing for big chain stores which are very strict in their requirements.
- What quantity of material will be delivered each week? Be realistic about your storage capacity.
- The company should be fully insured for loss, theft and fire risk while the goods are in your home. This should not be your responsibility. It should also be insured for goods in transit, even if you are fetching and carrying the goods yourself. If the company does not insure them, look elsewhere.
- Does your tenancy/mortgage/insurance allow this sort of work? If you are a council tenant you should be aware that certain local authorities require homeworkers to have written permission from them to do work at home. Most tenancy agreements prohibit the use or storage in the home of any inflammable materials, liquids, gases or chemicals, other than those normally required for household jobs. Consequently, be wary of any homework which requires you to glue, paint or spray. If a fire broke out in your home and such materials were found to be present it would undoubtedly invalidate your contents and building insurance.
- Will your neighbours object? Council tenants are usually prohibited in their lease from undertaking any activity that might cause a nuisance or inconvenience to neighbours. They may object to your receiving frequent deliveries by lorry of materials.

They may also object to any noise caused by machinery: some industrial sewing-machines can be very noisy.

- Will you be paid cash in hand, by cheque or direct to your bank account? Weekly, monthly or at the end of a period of seasonal work? Who will be paying tax and National Insurance: you or the company?

- Is the work seasonal? Some firms may take on out-workers only to meet the demand of the pre-season period.

- Ask if the company can offer you work all year round, even if it is of an entirely different nature. If not, try to get a precise idea of when the seasonal work will start and stop.

- Can you visit the factory? A company with nothing to hide should be pleased to allow factory visits. You can then see the processes which lead up to your work. It should also give you an opportunity to talk to some full-time workers and gauge whether the company has a good record.

- Does the work allow you to be flexible? You may be doing typing or invoicing at home and receiving daily deliveries or fax transmissions of material that needs to be tackled immediately. You can't cope with that if you have to attend to your family as well. Make sure you understand the schedule of any work that is on offer before you take it on.

- Does the employer/company provide you with equipment? There are various possibilities here.
  (a) You are provided with the necessary equipment and servicing back-up.

(b) You are provided with the equipment and asked to pay a deposit against it, which is refunded after a trial period. This is not ideal but understandable from the employer's point of view.

(c) You are asked to buy the equipment by having a small amount deducted from your wages each week. This is suitable only if the company wishes you to be self-employed and agrees that you can then use that equipment to do work for other companies. Check that the asking price is comparable to that of equipment available on the open market.

(d) You are expected to provide your own equipment. This is fair enough in the case of small items, but do not agree to buy major items outright.

- Do you have to buy anything else from the company? Some sales schemes expect participants to buy a case of samples. This is common practice and a reasonable safeguard against losing thousands of pounds' worth of stock.

- You need to know in advance whether you can take holidays or take a break for personal reasons, or pack up work for the children's school holidays without losing your chance to work for that company again.

Health and safety

You must not undertake any work which would be prejudicial to your own health and safety and, as you are working from home, that of your family. Some homeworking groups report that employers have given their homeworkers chemicals in unmarked tins and

31

jars. This is against the law. You should be informed as to exactly what substances you will be working with, how to handle them and what action to take to avoid illness or injury. For example, fumes from solvents and glues can cause headaches, dizziness, various allergies and heart and lung disease.

Similarly, working with fibres can cause health problems such as skin rashes, allergies and sore throats. Continual hunching over a sewing-machine can cause back, shoulder, neck and eye problems, while long hours in front of a VDU screen can cause eye strain, headaches, dizziness, nausea and muscle fatigue. Your local Environmental Health Department or relevant trade union will be able to supply you with information on how to avoid a range of work-related accidents or health problems.

Take sensible precautions

Good lighting, ventilation and seating, as well as frequent rest breaks, are very important for all types of repetitive work. Machinery and electrical equipment must have safety guards to minimise the risk of accident. You should confirm that your power supply is correctly protected and adequate for the task; also, that the company providing the machine has checked that it is safe.

You must have a separate, preferably lockable work room, particularly if you have children. Keep all flammable materials locked up outside the house, or in a lockable metal filing cabinet, and keep only the minimum necessary. Never smoke when dealing with flammable materials. Do not have your work room next to the children's bedrooms; in any case, ensure that the work room is properly ventilated to evacuate concentrations of fumes and dust. Do not store any flammable materials in a room that gets very warm. Keep plastic packaging materials away from small children and babies. If you are dealing with materials that increase the risk of fire, seek advice from the Fire Prevention Officer.

If you are engaged in sewing work, check that you are not scattering needles or pins around the house that could injure people or pets.

If you are worried about the effect that your work may be having on you or your family, discuss it with your work provider. If you get no help, contact your local Environmental Health Department or trade union.

What are your rights?

If you are a full-time employee you are entitled to:

- an itemised payslip, whether you receive your wages by cash, cheque or direct debit. This payslip should show gross wages and any deductions for tax, National Insurance, pension scheme etc., and your final net pay
- a contract of employment, stating the terms and conditions under which you are employed. This should be given to you within 13 weeks of your starting employment. It should detail pay, sick pay, holiday entitlements (if any), hours to be worked (perhaps a minimum or a maximum), the dates

when work is due to start and finish, the scale and rate of pay for piece work, and how often monies are to be paid

- maternity leave (of 14 weeks), regardless of length of service and hours of work, and the right to return to your job after the birth
- redundancy payment if you have worked for the same employer continuously for more than two years
- compensation for unfair dismissal, provided you can prove your claim, if you have worked for the same employer for more than two years
- a period of notice, depending on how long you have worked for the firm
- join a trade union if you wish, without being penalised by your employer
- equal pay, regardless of your sex or race, whether you work from home or at employer's premises.

If you work under 16 hours a week as an employee you are entitled to these rights after you have worked for the same employer for five years. (The last two items are automatic rights for any employee.)

If you are self-employed but in reality have done homework for one company for over two years for more than 16 hours a week, or for five years for more than eight hours a week, and you have kept a record of all your earnings, and a record of all the regular deliveries and collections of work from and to your home, you may be able to prove that you were, in fact, an employee and pursue a claim for redundancy or unfair dismissal if your work has stopped.

National Insurance and tax

If you are self-employed, read Chapter 6, which touches on the subjects of National Insurance and tax.

If you are an employee, NI and tax should be deducted from your wages by your employer if you earn over a certain amount each week. If you earn less than that you are exempt from NI.

Self-assessment

All taxpayers are now obliged by law to keep records of their income and capital gains to enable them to complete a tax return. These have to be kept, usually until 22 months after the end of the tax year to which they relate.

Self-employed people will have to hold on to the records of their income and capital gains for five years after the fixed filing date. They can calculate their own tax, or the Inland Revenue will do it free of charge. Many self-employed people have an accountant who will do this for them anyway.

Booklets explaining self-assessment can be obtained from the Inland Revenue.

THE IMPORTANCE OF MARKET RESEARCH

If you are still in the process of choosing an occupation or business idea to pursue at home, market research is an essential part of your decision-making. Finding out the right kind of information will aid you to make the right decisions when starting out; it will help you to invest wisely, and, later, it will enable you to keep ahead of the game.

Don't fall into the trap of thinking that this has nothing to do with you: the techniques for researching potential markets can be used by everyone and, in this information age where huge amounts of data are readily available in all forms, the lone individual can easily reap the benefits of some very expensive corporate research without going further than a library.

Where will my customers come from?

This is the burning question. You make a product, perhaps several products, or supply a service – where will you sell this product/service? To the general public, to specialist markets, to other businesses or to retail outlets? And will your market be local or more widely based?

Making the decision as to which market sector your product/service is aimed at is inextricably linked to how, eventually, you will reach the market you have targeted. An advertisement in the local paper may work if you are a gardener or a hairdresser but, even then, you might get work faster if you found out which people were most likely to want your product/service and addressed your sales pitch directly to them.

Sources of information

The first port of call has to be a reference or business library, where the librarians will help you wade productively through the information or, if they do not have it, to tell you what you need and where to get it. There are libraries in all sorts of places, such as hospitals, colleges and universities.

Good reference libraries stock all kinds of directories. You can find out, for example, how many craft/needlework magazines are published in the country (you could, perhaps, advertise in them, thereby reaching a specialist audience that would be interested in your products). A reference library should have the *Yellow Pages* directories for the whole country and you could photocopy the pages containing all the gift/craft shops and then do a mailshot to them all (selling your products on a regular basis through shops would give you some security). Most reference libraries stock a British Directory of Associations, which lists the officers of all kinds of associations that might be interested in your product.

Just a couple of hours' research could open up some promising markets, or show you that the product/service you are offering is not as marketable as you thought.

Libraries not only stock information in book form but on microfiche as well and also have access to the Internet. They may stock a whole year's back issues of trade or business magazines or national newspapers. You can look through them to see whether a particular topic of interest to you and relevant to your product/service has been covered in depth. Don't forget that any statistics published can be used in the marketing of your product.

Other sources of information are local Chambers of Commerce, Enterprise Agencies, regional branches of the Department of Trade and Industry and Training and Enterprise Councils (TECs). They can also help you with advice, give you literature, point you in the direction of companies that sell mailing lists for particular market sectors, and so on.

Conducting your own survey

British businesses spend millions of pounds each year getting professional researchers to conduct surveys. You can also conduct a modest survey of your own – it may pay surprising dividends.

First, get it clear in your mind exactly what you want to find out. If you are searching for an occupation and have not yet decided what it should be, perhaps you need to canvass house-to-house to find out what services people want? You need concise questions that prompt simple answers. For example:

- Do you employ a gardener?
- Would you like to employ a gardener?

- (If the answer to question 2 is yes) What jobs would you most want a gardener to do? Weeding/mowing the lawn/digging/repairing the fences/removing the rubbish/re-designing the garden.

From that simple questionnaire you might be able to ascertain that most people already employ a gardener. Alternatively, you may discover that most people would like to employ a gardener and that the job they most want doing is mowing the lawn.

Your next piece of market research is to find out what the competition is charging by telephoning a few gardeners and asking their prices. If you can undercut them and still make a living, print some leaflets offering lawn-mowing services at so much per hour and put them through the doors of the people you have surveyed.

Surveys don't have to be conducted door-to-door. You may be considering setting up a baby-sitting service, in which case you could ask the local mother and toddler groups, baby clinics, playgroups and nursery schools if they would distribute your survey and you would provide a box for collecting the completed surveys.

Perhaps you are planning to offer a car-valeting service. You could approach local companies and ask if you could survey the staff to see whether they would be interested in having their car valeted while they work.

Other ways of gathering information

You can find out lots of useful information by talking to

people and learning from the mistakes of others. Many craft workers, unfortunately, take a 'scatter gun' approach to marketing their wares, mainly by renting stalls at the many craft fairs held all over the country. This can often be a total waste of time and money.

Try to attend as many fairs as you can before choosing the venues and occasions that will genuinely increase your sales. Spend a day at a fair and watch the various stalls. You may note that certain items always sell quickly. Take note of the price ranges and what most people are prepared to pay for items. Listen to the public and note their comments. Look at the locations of the stalls. Does the stall nearest to the tea stand attract the most customers, or the one nearest the door? What display equipment do the busiest stalls have? Is there enough parking for everyone? All these factors have a bearing on whether a particular craft fair is a good marketplace for you.

Reading local newspapers is important. You can pick up some very useful information about market gaps from comments in the features or from the 'wanted' ads. Compile as much information as you can to help you make the right decisions at the beginning and continue to keep your 'market intelligence' up to date to help you make the right decisions in the future.

Researching working for someone else

A growing area of employment is as an agent, or subcontractor, for someone else. It is in fact self-employment, but in the case of subcontractors, someone else finds the work, and in the case of agents someone else manufactures the products which they sell.

Subcontracting

Subcontracting is becoming an increasingly common practice in trades apart from building. Take gardening: many successful gardening businesses start off as one-man/woman bands and, as they grow, require extra staff. Because the ability to carry out the work is dependent on the weather, it is risky to employ others and pay them to do nothing on rainy days, so subcontracting is the answer.

If you are a multi-skilled and fit person, able to turn your hand to any labouring job, whether it is digging, mixing concrete, carrying bricks or cleaning windows, do some research and find out which firms in your area employ subcontractors. You can then make yourself known to a variety of companies and get yourself put on their books for casual work.

If you have a special skill, find others with similar skills who have been operating longer than you and may be in a position to give you some of their overflow work. Or you might suggest to people with an allied skill that they offer their customers an extra service or product which you can provide when required. This will add an extra dimension to their business without their having to employ another person.

Agencies

An agent is a commission-only salesperson who sells

products for one or more manufacturers. Many people are involved in this type of work, from the women who sell cosmetics and jewellery through catalogues among friends to the thousands involved in network marketing schemes selling household products.

At the top end of the market are manufacturers' agents represented by the Manufacturers' Agents' Association* (MAA) of Great Britain. They are mainly people with a professional sales background and a great many contacts which they have built up over the years. However, no matter how good their contacts are, they still have to do the kind of research described here in order to add to their sales and to develop new lines. There is also a British Agents Register* which puts agents in touch with manufacturers.

Researching the job market

Finding home-based work of the general kind is not quite so easy. First, turn to the local paper to see if there are any advertisements offering work. The local Enterprise Agency may have advised recently established businesses which are thinking of employing outworkers. Also contact them, along with your local Trading Standards Department, to check whether a particular employer is blacklisted for any reason.

Disabled people can contact RADAR,* which publishes several factsheets and can refer you to other organisations that may have sources of work. Most JobCentres have a Disability Employment Adviser who will be able to advise on home-based opportunities.

MONEY – HOW TO RAISE IT

5

You will need some money behind you, if only to cushion you against the bad weeks. You may not need much of an initial investment in stock, materials or equipment but it helps your confidence if you know that you are not completely without money.

Bank loans take some time to be approved, loans from government sources and allied bodies take much longer and grants can take forever to come through. So you either have to be prepared to hang on to your full-time job while everything is processed, or you have to borrow the money.

Do not, however frustrated you are, borrow money from a money lender or finance house charging high rates of interest – you will cripple your venture before it even gets off the ground. Also, unless you have an interest-free loan or grant confirmed on paper and therefore can definitely pay someone back, do not borrow from friends or relatives. Borrowing money is the quickest way to damage a relationship.

Work out your needs

However modest your enterprise, draw up a business plan to help you to understand what your financial needs are likely to be and to show to anyone from whom you may be trying to borrow money.

A business plan is a concise report explaining your business – what it is and how it will make money – and providing a financial forecast.

What is your business?

Explain exactly what it is. If you are selling cosmetics door-to-door don't call it a beauty consultancy. If you are using an umbrella term – for example, you are a teleworker who is running a data management service – explain that this covers creating and amending mailing lists, keeping personnel records etc. on computer.

Why have you chosen this business?

If it is relevant, outline your experience in this field, your training and qualifications. If none of that is relevant, and you have decided on a business just because the potential is good and you need no training, explain that too.

What is the market for your product/service?

Explain what your market research has uncovered. If you can throw in a few statistics and name the sources, all the better. If you have done a survey in your local area, translate that into percentages for the report – for example, out of 54 households interviewed 47 per cent said that they were looking for a window cleaner, 23 per cent already had one, and the rest cleaned their own windows.

Have you identified the competition?

Do you know who else is offering the same product or service and is likely to affect your market? Or have you found a genuine market gap? Are you sure it is a gap? Has anyone tried to fill it before and come unstuck? Perhaps there is healthy competition but the market is continually growing – for example, there are plenty of other childminders but you have ascertained that the demand is so great that it outstrips the supply.

Why is your product/service better?

Take the example of a children's day nursery. Maybe you want to be better than the others and charge more, so you need to borrow money to put better equipment in the nursery garden and refurbish the bathrooms. In order for you to arrive at this decision you need to understand what the market wants and to identify what the competition is offering.

How will you reach your customers?

List all the ways in which you want to market your work and how often you would wish to run marketing exercises in the first year. You need to be able to quote the costs of advertising, leaflet printing, distribution and so on and then add this into your financial forecast, which is part 2 of your business plan (see below).

How much can you achieve on your own?

You have to be realistic about your capacity for work and exactly how much revenue you can generate. If you are doing the selling and the paperwork as well you will have only so much time to make your products or provide your service. If you make a variety of products, list them and explain how much time it takes to make each one and what the profit margin is.

Product	Time to make	Cost of materials	Selling price
Patchwork cot quilts	3 hours	£3.50	£10
Patchwork bags	2 hours	£2.50	£8
Patchwork bed quilts	20 hours	£25	£120

Someone who is considering giving you a loan may advise you that some items are not cost-effective and that you should concentrate your efforts on certain products only.

When will you need to expand?

You may need to use outworkers or take on someone part-time at the outset or you may be planning to employ someone else, if all goes well, in about a year's time. This needs to be explained.

What equipment do you have or need?

You may not have any equipment as such, or you may have old equipment that needs replacing. Perhaps you need to invest in another piece of equipment to allow you to diversify.

Who are or will be your suppliers?

Where do you buy or intend to buy your raw materials? Have you investigated the best prices? Can you get special deals? Anyone contemplating lending you money will be impressed if you can show that you have looked into all the possibilities.

Financial forecasts

The potential lender needs to know what money is going to go out of your business and what money is going to come in, so work this out with an accountant. You only need something quite simple – a sales forecast and a cash-flow forecast.

The sales forecast will involve a large element of hope. You must show if your sales are likely to be seasonal. For instance, a Christmas card manufacturer may have a lot of cash going out during the first year and not much coming in until the first quarter of the following year.

A cash-flow forecast is a complete breakdown of sources of income as well as expenses. The crucial point about a cash-flow statement is that it shows the timing of receipts and outgoings. It is perfectly possible for a business to look profitable but then fail because of adverse cash flow. Working from home means that you may put down a proportion of your rent/mortgage, and bills for light, heat and phone. Then there are items like petrol and car maintenance so that you can sell and deliver your goods. Also include any up-front investment that needs to be made in equipment or publicity, as well as any money that will need to be spent later to continue to publicise your business.

This exercise should be done in conjunction with costing your work. After you have done these figures you should be able to see whether or not your planned venture will be able to make a profit. If not, abandon the idea or see whether you can adapt it.

Decide what type of finance you need. A grant would be ideal, but you may not be able to get one. Perhaps you could get a bank loan or an overdraft facility to cover you for those periods when money is going out faster than it comes in.

A bank or an Enterprise Agency will go through the finished plan with you and discuss any weak points before you present it to the ultimate source of finance. It is an important part of your preparation and you must get it right. It is also a document you can build upon and re-present at a later date if necessary.

Once your business is under way, you will need to review and revise your financial forecast on a regular basis.

Raising money quickly

Earning money at home is all about careful planning and exercising caution. You must not rush into anything without thinking carefully about your course of action. However, there can be occasions when a business opportunity, vehicle or piece of equipment becomes available and, in order to grab it, you can't wait for lengthy financial procedures to be completed.

- Sell something – you could sell your car and get a cheaper one.
- Hire purchase – this is a good way of getting some essential equipment for your enterprise, if such an arrangement is available. Only opt for *bona fide* hire purchase agreements, after thoroughly investigating the true cost. Can you afford the repayments?
- Interest-free credit – this may be available on certain items. It is a good bargain, provided you can pay at the end of the free credit period.
- Credit card – buying items of equipment on a credit card will give you up to 56 days interest-free before the bill must be paid. It is an expensive way to buy as the interest rates are high if you do not settle the whole sum when you get the bill, but this form of credit can still be cheaper than a bank overdraft in the short term.
- Surrender a life insurance policy – only certain policies can be surrendered, and remember that if you do surrender you will lose out on the terminal bonus.
- Take out an insurance policy loan – this form of loan against policies from insurance companies has become very competitive but you have to have a suitable policy – an investment-type policy that is reasonably mature and one that is not linked to your mortgage.

49

The grants maze

Ideally, you should have planned your work-at-home career sufficiently to be able to have saved some money to start yourself off. At least allow yourself time to start up, so that you are not in a position of having to raise cash quickly. If you have planned ahead, you can apply for some of the many grants that are available.

Reference libraries hold publications which detail the grants that are available, through UK sources and the EC. Librarians should be able to access up-to-date grant information via their on-line databases. Also, your local Enterprise Agency or TEC will be able to tell you what, if anything, your enterprise may be able to gain.

What the banks and building societies can offer

Most lending institutions will expect you to bank with them if you want financial help. However, if your existing bank won't give you a loan or isn't offering a good package, you can apply to other institutions and offer to move your account.

Overdrafts

An overdraft is a good way for a new business venture to borrow money in the short term to finance the difficult cash-flow periods. The banks usually offer a fixed-fee overdraft where, on top of the interest charges, a monthly administration fee is levied, agreed in advance and set for a period of 12 months. Overdrafts should not be used in place of a loan to finance capital purchases.

Loans

'Short-term' loans of up to five years are available from banks. Rates of interest vary and can be fixed or can fluctuate with base rate. Fixed-rate loans are usually for a fixed period at an agreed rate of interest and a fixed repayment schedule. Shop around to see which lender offers the best deal. For financing the purchase of equipment a short-term loan usually works out cheaper than hire purchase or leasing, but you may be able to get a cheaper deal on hire purchase through an arrangement made by your local trade association.

ORGANISING YOURSELF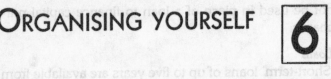

Try to make one particular place your work base. This does not mean that you cannot sit in front of the television doing your envelope-stuffing, but it does mean that you should have a place where everything is put away. And, if you have small children, that place should preferably have a lock on it for their safety and your sanity. However, try not to make one part of your house exclusively for work, as you may find yourself liable to pay business rates. (Storing away dangerous or valuable equipment in a lockable room is different.)

The place you set aside for most of your work should be comfortable, the temperature should be adjustable, there should be some natural light and good ventilation. In your enthusiasm at starting your own venture you may think that you can happily work in a damp cellar or a cold shed, but after a few weeks the reality will begin to get you down.

If you intend to do a lot of office work, you will require a proper office set-up. You will need space to lay out all your papers; a good desk and supportive chair; somewhere to file all your documents; a telephone; and peace and quiet if necessary.

If you are manufacturing, repairing, renovating, or raising plants in your outbuildings, you need some space and a source of power for your tools and to provide warmth and light, also an answering machine or a mobile/cordless telephone. The outbuilding should be waterproof and easily heated.

You may be able to do certain work anywhere, but you still need dry/animal/insect/children-proof accessible storage facilities.

Keeping accounts

You must keep a record of all financial transactions concerned with your work, not only to check whether you are making a profit or loss but also because the Inland Revenue and Customs and Excise can ask at any time to see accounts from six years previously, or longer if they suspect fraud.

As soon as you start to earn or pay out any money, keep a record of all expenses and payments as they arise. Make sure that the full date is on everything. Fill in cheque stubs and paying-in slips clearly and fully.

A simple ruled cash book may be enough to start with: on one side enter what you have earned and on the other enter expenses, with dates and any other relevant details. Keep distinct records of cash and banking transactions. All money received should be paid in, even if you withdraw it again immediately. You must keep all receipts, till slips, invoices etc., so that an auditor can check them against your accounts.

The records kept will be dictated by the volume of work involved. For instance, a writer whose year's work produces, say, one book may just have a single receipt of payment from the publisher, with few expenses. On the other hand, a hairdresser will have numerous small receipts of cash and expenses for stock, equipment and telephone, and will need a more elaborate cash book.

Write up your account books at least once a week. Where applicable, the following should be recorded, with dates:

- payments made for stock
- payments made for other purchases or services
- money received and from whom
- goods or services supplied and from whom
- cash drawn for personal use.

Although records can be simple, they must be comprehensive and capable of providing information for income tax purposes and for VAT (or, if VAT registration is not yet required, capable of being adapted later to provide the required information).

If you decide that more elaborate records are necessary, go to an office equipment shop and examine the cash record books and account books available. Many accountants recommend using something like a Simplex D cash book. Or, if you have a computer, you could choose one of the many accounting software packages. Keep back-up copies of all computer accounts in a separate place.

File all your invoices, bills, copies of receipts given, cheque stubs, letters and anything else in date order. If there are not many, they can be put into a folder or box file or on a spike; or keep them in a ring binder, numbered and cross-referenced to your account books.

Separate the papers for each accounting year so that when you come to make your declaration of income for tax purposes you will have all the relevant material to hand.

Make a note of any item that might be allowable for tax purposes. It is difficult to get a claim allowed for items not recorded in the business books.

Be especially careful to record all expenses that relate to your work where part of your business expenses come out of the household account, such as electricity or telephone bills. You will need some record of all such expenses when compiling a claim for tax allowances.

The money that comes in and goes out for your work should be kept strictly separate from your personal and household finances. You could have two cheque books and paying-in books, using one for business and one for private payments, or you could simply mark all personal transactions in the accounts – say as 'drawings' for items of personal expenditure, if you are self-employed.

You could open a separate account for your business finances, or an instant access building society account. (But make sure you do not pay two lots of bank charges – most banks charge for each transaction unless you keep your current account in credit to a certain sum.)

If you are self-employed or starting to run a business in a very small way you may want to avoid opening a special 'business' bank account because you will be charged more for the privilege. If you start to expand your operation and require more assistance from a bank, then is the time to transfer to a business account. Even if you are just a personal account holder you are entitled to ask for regular monthly statements, or more frequent ones if you wish, although you will be charged for any service that is not standard. Check at regular intervals that the balance of your account agrees with your account books.

It is essential to set aside in a savings deposit account the money required to meet tax (and VAT) liabilities when these fall due.

Employing an accountant

It may be worth getting an accountant or book-keeper to advise you on the best method of keeping accounts and how to claim any expenses allowable against tax for the self-employed. Personal recommendation is a good way of finding such an adviser, or look in the *Yellow Page* or local trade directories, or find out the address from the local library of your nearest district society of chartered or certified accountants. The society will be able to give you some names and details of particular accountants' specialities.

When first contacting a firm, make it clear that you need somebody who knows about the financial aspects of a self-employed or freelance person. An accountant with particular knowledge of self-employment can save you a lot of money as well as time.

Accountants charge on an hourly basis, according to seniority and type of work, plus expenses. There is no fixed scale, but allow for at least £25 an hour, plus VAT. Specify in writing what work you want an accountant to do for you and ask what his or her charge is likely to be. The bill should be itemised according to the work you have agreed between you – for example, giving advice, preparing a tax return, dealing with VAT and any other book-keeping matters. The more careful your own book-keeping, the less work an accountant has to do and the more money you will save.

The accounting year

With the possible exception of the first year, your accounts should run for a 12-month period which begins and ends on the same dates each year. Your accounting year need not necessarily be the calendar year 1 January to 31 December, nor need it coincide with the tax year 6 April to 5 April.

Because of the way in which self-employed tax assessments are made, substantial tax advantages or disadvantages can result from the selection of the annual accounting date.

If you end your accounting year a little after the start of the tax year, you will maximise the period of time between making the profits and paying the final instalment of tax due on them. As long as your profits are rising, this is an advantage, as you will be paying tax on lower profits than you are currently making. Take advice from your accountant and/or refer to *Which? Way to Save Tax* (published annually by Which? Ltd/ Consumers' Association).

Tax and submitting accounts

The Inland Revenue has a large range of publications that cover many aspects of tax and most types of business from keeping livestock to renting rooms; get its free catalogue of leaflets and booklets. In one of its publications, *Getting Tax Right From the Start*, it offers a clear guide as to what you should keep and record, such as all business receipts and earnings; day-to-day expenditure; capital expenditure; and the details of the purchase and sale of capital equipment.

If you are genuinely self-employed, you will be taxed under Schedule D. This may allow you to claim tax relief on more expenses than if you were an employee and taxed by PAYE under Schedule E and also means that you pay less National Insurance. It is important that the Inland Revenue has accepted your self-employed status, because if it hasn't some of your clients might make you pay employer's contributions.

To be considered self-employed, you have to prove to the taxman's satisfaction that no one person has the sole rights to your working time. Therefore, try to get work from several sources.

Whether you are employed or self-employed depends on the terms of the particular engagement you have entered into. If you supply a service to only one, or predominantly one customer, a formal letter or contract might clarify your position as an independent self-employed contractor. The Inland Revenue leaflet *Employed or Self-Employed?* offers guidance on the subject.

This will also have a bearing on what sort of National Insurance contributions you should pay. Check with the DSS if you are in any doubt about the contributions you should be making and read its literature before starting your venture or seeking work.

It is possible for a person to be in the situation of being both employed and self-employed, for example as an employed teleworker but doing some freelance work too, in which case Class 1 and 2 contributions together will be limited to no more than the maximum contributions an employee would pay. But you may have to pay Class 4 contributions on top.

Self-employed people are exempt from paying National Insurance contributions if:

- they are in receipt of maternity allowance
- they are sick for a prolonged period
- they have reached pensionable age
- earnings for that year are below a certain limit.

Note that Class 4 contributions are related to profits and if you should make a loss in any taxable year you will not pay income tax or Class 4 contributions.

VAT

Registration for VAT is compulsory if your sales for the preceding 12 months or your anticipated sales for the next 12 months are over the current VAT threshold of £48,000. Some traders register voluntarily for VAT even though their sales do not come above the threshold because it is advantageous for them to be able to reclaim the VAT they pay out on supplies. For more information, consult Customs and Excise.

Insurance

If you are contemplating earning money from home,

talk to your insurance company. You will certainly need a special policy to cover any business equipment, tools and other items necessary to your trade. You need not only to insure them against theft, fire and other hazards but also against breakdown and the consequential loss of business while they are being repaired or replaced.

What you pay for your insurance depends very much upon what business you are engaged in. There are some off-the-shelf packages which cover particular trades, but read the fine print to make sure that every aspect of your operation is covered. Computer insurance, for example, is only of value if it covers the data (which may be your most valuable asset) as well as the hardware and software. If your house or workshop should burn down or be destroyed in a storm, you need to be able to rent somewhere else while repairs are being done, so this should be an integral part of your cover.

Some professional bodies and national associations have negotiated special insurance packages on behalf of their members.

Your insurance company will also be able to advise on the four important areas of public liability, product liability, professional indemnity and employer's liability, where appropriate. Don't forget that you may need other types of insurance such as private medical insurance, the right kind of car insurance and keyman insurance.

Costing your work

What you can charge for your product or services very much depends upon what the customer is prepared to pay and what the competition is charging for the same product or service.

You may have little choice in this matter. If you are a hairdresser, you know that your clients will pay only £X for a shampoo and set; if you run a driving school you know that your customers will pay only £Y for a driving lesson.

So you have to start from the point where you know how much you will charge and why. The question is, can you make a profit? You then have to look at all your costs and see whether they are sufficiently low to enable your product/service to make you a profit. If not, can they be lowered? If they cannot, you have problems.

It may be that you are not restricted in what you can charge for your product or service because it is something new, unique or rare and the customers may be prepared to pay highly for it.

Having decided which of these applies to your business, you can return to the conventional method of assessing your cost structure. It is an exercise which should be done very early on, before you start your venture. You will certainly need to do it if you are going to present a business plan to a lending institution, but it is advisable to do it anyway as you will arrive not only at a cost structure but also at an operating budget – that is to say, you will know how much you can afford to spend on certain items and whether your business will make a satisfactory profit.

Fixed costs

These are the costs that don't vary with the amount you produce – in other words, you have to pay them even if you produce nothing at all. Write down a list that includes (for a full year) any business rates (don't forget that, even working from home, you could be liable to pay business rates), electricity (on top of your household consumption), telephone rental, loans, insurances and equipment hire.

Variable costs of goods

Next assess the costs to your business which fluctuate according to the amount you produce, for example, the materials you purchase to make your product, the packaging, and any seasonal labour.

This is a complex sum. Basically, you have to assume a realistic figure for goods that you will hope to produce and sell in your first year. Let us say that you are making soft toys and you plan to work alone for the first year. You buy your material from a wholesaler. You know that £60-worth of material enables you to make 100 soft toys in one month, which you would sell at £10 each.

Make a list of your variable costs that includes (for a full year) materials, transport including petrol, postage on regular mailshots, telephone and fax costs, repairs to machinery.

Add the two sets of costs together, and divide the total by the number of soft toys you can make in one year. Say each toy costs £4.32 to make – if you sell them for £10 you should produce a healthy profit.

However, bear in mind that these figures are only basic illustrations. Any accountant would advise that you must build into your calculations hidden costs such as waste of materials, depreciation of equipment and any periods of illness when you cannot produce toys.

Other factors could influence your profit margin, for example:

- rise in petrol costs
- rise in postage costs
- rise in costs of materials
- competition forces down the market prices
- regular sales outlets lose interest in your product
- you need to make a large investment in equipment
- your customers force you to offer credit card facilities
- you acquire some bad debts
- you are forced to find money for legal fees.

Some of these can be built in at the planning stage. If you know, from the above calculations, what your basic profit margin will be, then you will have to allocate some of that hoped-for profit towards a contingency fund for those unexpected expenses. You should also engage in some costing exercises for possible future scenarios, such as diversification.

Diversification

Let us assume that you have your finger on the pulse of the marketplace and you feel confident that you can produce soft toys that meet current trends: for example, all the kids are mad about trolls, so you decide to manufacture trolls for a few months, in addition to your regular line. First you have to investigate the costs of the materials required to make the new product, but you find that your new basic product cost is £4.47, so your profit margin has been eroded by 15p.

Whether to diversify or not is a 'Catch 22' situation. If you are still going it alone, then, on paper, all you are succeeding in doing is shaving 15p off your profit. But you may be in the position of not having any choice. If you don't offer what the market wants, it is eventually going to get tired of your basic range of soft toys and you will lose sales anyway.

Pricing a service

Again, you are probably restricted by the current market rate for your service. Customers will pay no more and you may not be able to afford to undercut that. Take the example of a word processor operator working from home. Can you undercut the current going rate? It is difficult to price a service but you still have to add up your fixed and variable costs and find out how many hours of work you need a year in order to at least cover costs, and then you know what to aim beyond.

Other factors in pricing

Many external factors can contribute to changes in costs and, therefore, changes in your prices, so the costing/pricing exercise has to be repeated at frequent intervals. Here are some of the factors to be aware of.

- **Interest rates** – the interest rates on loans and mortgages can change. You may be lucky enough to have negotiated fixed rates for a couple of years and therefore those portions of your fixed costs will stay put for that period, but most people are subject to the rise and fall of interest rates.
- **Child care** – working at home and looking after your children may not be feasible once you get a large quantity of orders/contracts/commissions.
- **Other fixed costs** – insurance premiums will rise, as will the cost of telephone, electricity and gas, postage, petrol and so on. While insurance premiums may rise only once a year, items like petrol can become more expensive at any time.
- **Costs of materials** – your suppliers will pass on any of their rising costs to you. You could also be in a position where your main supplier ceases trading and you have to find another more expensive source.
- **Customer demand** – success doesn't always mean more profits. Generating a greater volume of goods means incurring more costs. The bulk-buying customer may also demand a discount, which you feel unable to refuse, and this obviously affects your general cost/price structure. On the other hand,

demand may peter out and you find that you have to diversify into other products or services, re-market them and incur a whole new set of costs, not necessarily greater but certainly different.

- **Time constraint** – you may manufacture products that have a limited 'shelf-life' – seasonal goods that have to be sold before the relevant holiday, goods that celebrate particular anniversaries, goods that cater to a children's craze. Once the marketing opportunity is gone, the merchandise has to be sold at a greatly reduced price. The wastage of stock has to be built into the initial pricing decision.
- **Increased competition** – if your competitors start slashing prices you could be in trouble unless you have allowed some margin for discount right from the beginning. This is why it is important before trading to work out in detail the profit you need to make on each unit (product or hour of service) in order to survive.

Budgeting

In order to decide how much income to aim for, by costing your work and fixing a price, you need to draw up a budget for the forthcoming year. You have to look at your fixed costs and decide, before you commit them to the business plan, whether they can be reduced at all. Don't forget to include any expenditure on machinery or equipment.

With the variable costs, you have to ensure that your supply is the cheapest and/or the best and that the supply is safe and/or you have a back-up source of supply.

Cash flow

This is the most important part of your budgeting exercise because it shows money movements in and out of your account. It will show when you will be paying bills each month or quarter, and when, you hope, money will be coming in.

This is inextricably linked to your marketing strategy because how you choose to sell your goods determines the way in which your income is generated.

Say you make preserves. Half your stock is sold to farm shops – you bill them when you deliver the order and you give them 30 days in which to pay, so every 30 days a certain amount of money will be coming into your account. The other half of your stock you sell every week at a market, so a certain amount of money is coming in every week.

One of the most dangerous things is to **have** too much stock, either in production or finished but in your home, or out with customers, and no money due in for a long period. If you are a small producer you cannot afford to incur a lot of costs on materials, time and labour without an immediate return. It is better to produce and sell little and often at first.

Halfway through your first year your accountant or bank manager should be able to look at your books and compare them with your original budget. This will show whether your original estimates of work and sales were accurate. If they differ greatly, things have worked out better than expected or things are going wrong. This is the time for analysis as to how you proceed for the rest of the year and beyond.

Formal quotations

Sometimes you may be asked to give a formal quote on price before the potential customer will place a definite order. A quotation is a legally binding document which could be used against you if you failed to keep to its terms, so you have to be absolutely clear in your written quotation exactly what you are offering for the price you are asking.

Make a realistic estimate first of how long the job will take you and what expenses, if any, you will incur in order to do the job. Say you are dressmaker who has been commissioned to make a wedding dress. You have discussed with the customer what type of dress she wants. Will it be straightforward or will she want hand embroidery? Does she want one of your existing patterns or will you have to design something just for her? Who will provide the material? Will she come to you for fittings or will you have to go to her, which will cost you time and money?

Having sorted out the preliminary details, quote as follows:

- State exactly what service you are offering, e.g. designing the dress as well as making it.
- State who is providing materials. Emphasise that whatever arrangement is agreed, the material is of the customer's choice.
- How long you will take to do the job. (Put in the phrase 'unforeseen circumstances excepted' – that covers you if some disaster occurs.)

- How many fittings you will require to complete the job.
- The price you are quoting.
- How long that price will stand, i.e. how long the customer has to make up her mind before the price goes up.
- If it is relevant, reserve the right to alter the price should the cost of the basic materials go up, or the customer demands a change in the dress.
- Say whether the price is inclusive or exclusive of VAT, if that pertains to your business.
- Payment terms, i.e. when the customer has to pay for the job. In this case, payments should be spread throughout the period of the job, with the first payment covering the complete cost of the materials so that you are not out of pocket should the customer disappear. It would be wise not to purchase the materials until this first payment has been made.
- Cancellation fee: in order to cover your time and effort you should state that once an order is placed by the customer the job cannot be cancelled without some charges being incurred.
- Finally, ask for the customer's acceptance in writing. It may expedite matters if you include in your quotation an acceptance sheet which the customer just has to sign and return. It could read as follows:

I have read the enclosed quotation and I accept the terms and conditions. I enclose the first payment of £XX.
Signature
Date

Tendering

This is just another way of quoting for a job, except that you definitely know that you are competing for a job because several others will have been asked to tender. It is a common practice for, say, consultants or office service bureaux – any business that sells to other businesses.

None of the companies or individuals tendering a price will know what prices they are competing against. It is not always the lowest tender that is accepted, as other factors can have a bearing.

Never tender an impossibly low price for a job, no matter how desperate you are. You have to cover your costs at least. Never undervalue your time or expertise – it will only arouse suspicion.

If, after the tendering process, you find that you did not get the job, ask why. If several companies tell you that your price was too high, review your pricing structure. It may just be that you are competing against people who have a bigger profit margin than you, because of lower overheads, more resources and so on and can afford to quote lower prices. Then you must review your own service and see if you can offer a different, higher-value product.

MARKETING YOUR WORK   8

The whole idea of marketing (and public relations) is that you should never rest on your laurels. You have to keep carrying out research, anticipating any changes, developing new markets and continuing to impress your customers with your efficiency, enthusiasm and determination. The image that you project, however small your operation, is an important part of the business of attracting custom.

There are several methods of selling products and services from your home:

- **Putting a postcard in a shop window** – a useful way of drawing attention to your service in a small community but not recommended as the sole form of selling.
- **Calling door to door with the products in hand** – this may be suitable for a small selection of reasonably lightweight products which might instantly appeal to a person at home during the day. You need to have a car or van close at hand, so that you can keep topping up your hand-carried selection of goods.
- **Delivering leaflets door to door (or car to car)** – the leaflets advertising your service or product have to be eye-catching, the message punchy and the contact information very clear. Leaflets stuck under wind-

71

screen wipers have a tendency to blow away or be thrown away. Sometimes it is better to hand out leaflets at a strategic point – say the exit to a car park.

- **Delivering catalogues door to door** (and returning to collect them) – this is double the work but you will eventually build up a round of regular customers. The products have to be of limited life span, like cosmetics or household cleaners, otherwise you will not generate regular sales.

Selling to retailers

Quite often, craftworkers and artists find that shops will take their work initially on a sale-or-return basis, and then place regular orders. Having several retail outlets can provide a bedrock of regular income which leaves you free to sell in other ways that do not compete with the retail outlets.

Selling through your own retail outlet

Many people take a stall at a craft fair or market as a first exercise in marketing. It has the advantage that you don't have to pay anyone else to sell for you but you probably have to pay for the stall space. It is of least advantage to a manufacturer because time taken to man a stall for a few hours, plus the loading and unloading, is time taken away from manufacturing. This type of marketing really works best for those who sell other people's products: for example, they go to wholesale outlets and buy clothes to sell on at a profit.

Women's Institute (WI) Co-operative Markets are a good place at which to sell home-made, home-grown and hand-crafted goods. New producers do not have to be WI members, but they do have to become share-holders in the County Market Society. WI markets are true co-operatives and everyone is expected to help run their market. The Women's Institute Head Office* can supply further information.

Some craftworkers or caterers manufacture products all week and then sell them at fairs or markets at the weekend. This is fine if the sales generated justify using up all your free time, and if you have other sales out-lets, but very dispiriting to keep packing and unpacking the same products and selling just a few items here and there.

Advertising your product in the press

Advertising needs to be carefully targeted so that you don't waste money. There has to be a certain amount of experimentation and you have to analyse the results in order to gauge the return you are getting. If you manu-facture a product or provide a service to a specialist mar-ket you will have discovered, during your market research, those publications which cover that market.

By comparing circulations and rates, you will be able to assess the ones you think will give you the best response. You then need to study them and find what you think are the best positions for your advertisements. Perhaps you would like your advertisement to be oppo-site an article that relates to the sort of product or service you are offering, or under a special heading in the clas-sified section? Negotiate with the advertising department of the publication. Take advantage of any special offers.

Generally, one advertisement alone will not give you a true picture of whether that medium works for you or not. Three consecutive advertisements are considered to be the normal 'try-out' period. By the end of that you will know whether to invest in more advertisements or try something else.

You could take some advice from an advertising agent. A reputable local company will be able to give you preliminary recommendations on where best to advertise and will suggest a starting budget. Make sure that the company understands the modest size of your overall budget at the outset.

Delivering samples to an office or factory

There are certain products that people need to examine at leisure, like books or pieces of china. You need to find a sympathetic person at the workplace who will take charge of your products and then collect the orders for you – perhaps you could offer them a free gift of one of the products. The advantage of this method is that it leaves you free to pursue other things and you have a large captive market looking at your products for a few days. Make sure that the boss is in agreement.

Selling through a party scheme

The party scheme works quite simply but is heavily reliant on the host or hostess being able to gather a large group of friends; also, you or your agent have to be present. You need to advertise, perhaps in the local newspaper, for party hosts and to vet the applications by visiting the intended party venue. It's not going to be very productive if the person lives in a very small house because you won't be able to display your products properly and there won't be enough people present to make it worthwhile. Also, the person hosting the party should have the sort of friends who are likely to be interested in and able to afford your product.

Getting orders by word of mouth

This works for some people, particularly those who produce commissioned work such as sculptures, tapestries or furniture. You may have a business where news of your abilities spreads from friend to friend until you cannot take on any more jobs. However, this is not a marketing strategy upon which anyone should base their future prospects. Even someone who has lots of clients from the start should aim at some point to glean new clients via a different route.

Joining a professional body

This is a must for consultants of all kinds, because membership means that you appear on any membership lists or in any directories that are sent out to interested parties. It also means that you have access to the right markets through the organisation's mailing list and newsletter or magazine.

When do you need help?

You can take advantage of marketing advice and help at any time, if you can afford it, but there are certain areas where specialist help is essential.

Selling your reputation

This is for those individuals who initially sell themselves purely on the strength of their CV – for example, consultants who put themselves forward for freelance appointments, either on their own initiative or through an agency. Making one CV stand out from all the others is sometimes the job of an expert, usually a recruitment consultant, who can advise on the arrangement of information and the presentation of a CV to achieve maximum effect.

Free marketing advice and training

There is plenty of free advice to be had, but do some research so that you can pick the appropriate body that has an interest in your particular line of work.

The Training and Enterprise Councils (TECs, contactable through your local Enterprise Agency) in England and Wales and Local Enterprise Companies (LECs) in Scotland hold courses on 'How to research a market', 'Sales and marketing techniques' and 'How to plan marketing and selling' as part of their Train to Work/Self Start programme. They offer free advice, free training over the first year and financial assistance provided you are eligible.

Low-cost ways of promoting sales

The aim of public relations is to keep your name and product or service in front of the public. You don't even have to be self-employed to do this – lots of agents, selling on behalf of others, become involved in self-promotion as part of their marketing strategy. There are various cost-effective methods.

Sending out press releases

Compile a list of all the relevant media. A press release is just a simple story – no more than one page – about

76

something your business has achieved: a new product or service, an expansion, or some other event in which you are involved. Send a photograph too if appropriate. You would be surprised to know how often local newspapers print small stories about local business people just to fill space in a 'slow news' week.

Writing articles

If you are an expert on a particular subject related to your occupation, write articles about it for the trade or hobby press. Copies can be included in any sales literature sent out to potential customers. Insist that you are properly credited at the end of the article, for example: 'Mary Johnson runs a company from her home in Thistown called the Flower Tub; tel: XXX.'

Giving talks and lectures

Get yourself on to the lecture circuits. This may be through the Women's Institute, Townswomen's Guild or some other organisation looking for speakers on crafts, cookery or similar topics. Sports clubs are another outlet for after-dinner speakers. Professional institutes and business organisations such as chambers of commerce are always looking for speakers on business-related topics, as are Rotary Clubs and Round Tables.

The object is to give your talk and display your wares or sales literature at the same time, or hand round business cards.

Running workshops or giving demonstrations

If you grow flowers and dry them to sell to flower-arrangers and florists, run flower-arranging workshops or demonstrations and convert your pupils into customers at the same time.

Donating prizes to local competitions

Most local newspapers like to run competitions and are always looking for prizes. You could offer one in return for an article about your enterprise and perhaps a free advertisement. Insist that you receive all the entries to the competition, because you will then have the benefit of the names and addresses of people who, although they did not win your product, might like to buy it if you write an enticing letter.

Staging publicity stunts

You may specialise in knitting jumpers so perhaps you could, in conjunction with the WI, organise a knitting marathon for charity, making sure that your name is featured prominently in any publicity.

Sending 'free' gifts

The gifts, of course, are not free to you. It's a common practice in business to send valued customers a gift at Christmas of, say, a calendar or a pen – something that carries your name and phone number on it. It is not a bad public relations ploy to copy, if you can make something small and cheap that will encourage good customers to continue to buy from you.

Conclusion

In marketing (and public relations) you should never rest on your laurels. You have to keep plugging away at your markets, carrying out research, anticipating any changes, developing new markets and continuing to impress your customers with your efficiency, enthusiasm and determination. The image that you project, however small your operation, is an important part of the business of attracting custom.

GETTING EQUIPMENT, SUPPORT AND SKILLS

9

Whatever occupation you are involved in, it is essential to have equipment that will enable you to function as efficiently as possible. This may involve setting up any or all of the following: separate lines for domestic and business use; cordless telephone or a mobile; an answering machine; 'call waiting' service; a pager, a fax; a fax/photocopier; and a computer.

You might get by with a basic typewriter and a filing cabinet, but if your occupation involves any written reports, estimates, quotations or articles – anything that might need amending or updating, or any document that needs to be sent to several people – you would save time by investing in a computer.

If you buy a computer, there are several safeguards to remember:

- Keep the computer purely for business. Do not allow other members of the family to play games on it or to introduce other software that might contain a virus – it could wipe out your business records.
- Buy new disks that are marked 'guaranteed virus-free', and invest in virus-checking software if your computer doesn't already have this built into the system – every time you receive a disk from a client, say, you need to virus-check it before accessing it.

- Regularly copy all the material stored on your computer on to back-up disks so that in the event of fire or theft you can retrieve the information. Don't forget, it is not your computer that is indispensable to your business but your data – you can replace your computer straight away.
- Keep a set of paper records, filed in a different part of the house. You will in any case have to make copies of all your accounts materials in order to send them to the Inland Revenue (or VAT inspector).

Other equipment

What other sort of equipment you need will be determined by your initial market research. What do your competitors use? What manufacturing techniques do they employ? Can you afford to copy them?

If you have industrial equipment that performs any function that could injure or kill, safeguards are vital. You must be able to lock it away when you are not using it, and you must make sure that no one is able to operate it or allowed to stand near it when it is in use. If safety gear is appropriate you must have it handy and wear it whenever you use the machinery. Never be casual about it.

Have the equipment serviced regularly, particularly if a third party is involved. If you are a homeworker working for someone else, call in your employer if you have any doubts about the machinery. If you suspect a fault, switch off and do not use it again until it has been checked by a competent person.

Don't keep machinery that uses fuel in any part of the house, not even a scullery or conservatory. And don't keep photographic film or video tapes on open shelves – they can burn very fast and give off noxious fumes. Keep them in a fireproof, damp-proof cupboard away from the house. Ask your local Fire Officer for advice.

Buying equipment

Which? magazine* has published surveys on most kinds of domestic and office equipment, with test results on the level of performance you can expect for your money.

Specialist equipment may have been the subject of similar surveys by trade associations. It is worth enquiring whether the association relevant to your line of work has done tests on the type of equipment you intend to buy. Similarly, you can often find informative articles in trade magazines or papers.

You could also go to an independent dealer who stocks the makes of equipment that interest you. Go armed with a list of questions: you need to know exactly what you want from your piece of equipment so that the dealer will be able to make a positive recommendation.

- What do you want to do with it? How demanding are you going to be? Will you be using it all the time?
- Do you need to carry it around with you?
- Do you need it to be flexible? Do you need power tools, for example, to do the small intricate jobs as

well as the big hefty ones? Do you need equipment that is battery-operated, so that you can use it anywhere?

- Do you need something sophisticated or can it be simple?
- How much does the price of this piece of equipment vary? Is the price cheaper at certain times of the year? Is there a discount for cash? Some shops are prepared to forgo the percentage they would normally pay to a credit card company if you pay cash.
- Do you have to have accessories?
- Do you need to upgrade your machinery regularly?
- Do you have to buy, or would you be better hiring? Hiring can also be a better option if you need a piece of equipment for a short time only or you want to experiment by offering another product or service but don't want to commit yourself to buying machinery until you know there's a demand.
- What about back-up?
- Do you need an extended guarantee?

Insurance

Insure all your important equipment against damage or theft. You will need to replace it quickly to keep your business going.

GETTING SUPPORT

There are many sources of support that could help you with the financial, legal or marketing aspects of your business. For instance, some banks offer a 'small business adviser' (although their time and experience may be limited).

A solicitor can help a lone entrepreneur in many ways. Some firms publish a scale of charges for uncomplicated jobs, such as writing letters to bad debtors. For basic advice on contracts or consumer matters you can contact your local Citizens Advice Bureau.

Your local authority has plenty of literature available, covering a wide range of occupations, which explains the government and EC regulations that may apply, while trade and professional associations usually have legal departments which give advice to members on legal problems.

Above all, enlist the support of your family and friends. Apart from being extra pairs of hands when the workload piles up, they can also be good sources of information and fresh ideas. It is a common trap for individuals working from home to operate in a vacuum. Ideas become stale, problems get out of proportion, the ability to delegate disappears. Let others support you in whatever way they can and you will find that you get greater enjoyment from your work.

GETTING SKILLS

You may want to learn new skills to help you to diversify from the product or service range you are currently offering; alternatively, you may be acquiring a new piece of equipment which demands a period of training to acquaint yourself fully with its finer points.

There are many places to go for the necessary training: Adult Education Institutes (evening or day classes), universities or colleges (for full-time courses) or correspondence courses (for diplomas in a wide variety of skills). Other courses can be found by contacting the manufacturers of the equipment you want to buy or by visiting your local library, JobCentre, nearest Training Access Point (TAP) or TEC.

Training on specific pieces of equipment should be no problem, although it may not be a free service if it requires more than half a day's instruction. Many Adult Education Institutes run computer software courses which allow you to learn at a steady pace, perhaps before you invest in the relevant software. Many manufacturers offer training videos, often free of charge, with each new purchase.

If you are a craftworker who would like to add to your skills you can look in some of the art and crafts publications to see what courses are on offer or contact the Crafts Council.*

CUTTING THROUGH
THE RED TAPE

10

It can be dispiriting to someone who is simply developing a hobby into a business to find that once he or she starts selling to the general public a tidal wave of regulations looms, but it is best to find out about these sooner rather than later.

One of the best places to start is your local Trading Standards Office, which will have a Department of Regulatory Services (or similar). Even if you just have an idea at this stage, staff will be able to advise you on what regulations will come to bear on your enterprise.

If you are investigating selling your products through shops, the buyers will probably tell you what they are allowed to sell and how the goods should be packaged and labelled.

Start at the beginning

First, make sure that you are allowed to conduct your proposed enterprise from your home. Check your lease or mortgage and your house insurance. If the proposed business is allowable, in that it is not noisy, hazardous, likely to cause offence to the neighbours or require alteration to a listed building in a conservation area, the chances are that you will be able to proceed.

If you are going to change the use of your premises, change the shape or alter its appearance, you will have to ask for planning permission from your local authority.

Certain businesses may not operate without a licence: ask your local authority, which will redirect you if necessary.

Health and safety

This is probably the major area (particularly if you will be involved in the preparation of food) – and far too wide for the scope of this book – where you can fall foul of the law. You must be prepared to invest quite a bit of time, patience and money in getting it right. Make enquiries at the Environmental Health Office of your local authority first.

87

- **Toys** – the regulations covering the safety of children's toys are understandably extensive, not least in specifying certain categories of products that are not considered toys at all (e.g. children's jewellery, large jigsaws, detailed scale models, folk and decorative dolls and Christmas decorations), although these are subject to their own safety regulations. Note that lack of compliance with the Toy Regulations can mean six months' imprisonment or a fine of up to £2,000. For full details of how to go about making toys that can be sold legally, seek advice from your local Trading Standards Office.
- **Clothing** – the Department of Trade and Industry is very particular about the size and style of the print used on the labels, as well as advertisements, so if you are seeking to develop a clothing business, particularly if you will be making nightwear or baby-clothes, get as much advice as possible from your local Trading Standards Office.
- **Furniture** – as with toys, furniture and upholstery labels have to comply with EC standards and it is best to seek advice from your Trading Standards Office.

Acts of Parliament

Anyone who is making, selling or importing anything or providing any sort of service to the public needs to become familiar with the relevant parts of the Consumer Protection Act 1987 and/or the Supply of Goods and Services Act 1982. The Patents Act 1977 may also have some relevance to your work. The Data

Protection Act 1984 is essential reading for a self-employed teleworker, while those contemplating reproducing characters such as Paddington Bear and Noddy on goods should check the copyright position (permission will be needed). Your local reference library will supply further information.

ADDRESSES

Crafts Council
44A Pentonville Road,
London N1 9BY
0171-278 7700

Disability Alliance
Universal House,
88–94 Wentworth Street,
London E1 7SA
0171-247 8776

Manufacturers' Agents' Association
1 Somers Road, Reigate,
Surrey RH2 9DU
(01737) 241025

**RADAR (Royal Association for
Disability and Rehabilitation)**
12 City Forum, 250 City Road,
London EC1V 8AF
0171-250 3222

Telecottage Association
WREN Telecottage, Stoneleigh Park,
Warwickshire CV8 2RR
(01203) 696986

Which? Limited
Consumers' Association,
2 Marylebone Road, London NW1 4DF
0171-830 6000

**WI (Women's Institute) Country
Markets Ltd**
104 New Kings Road,
London SW6 4LY
0171-371 9300

INDEX

Other titles in this series

You and Your Doctor
Ever felt that there's an unnecessary barrier between you and your GP? This book explains what you are entitled to expect from your doctor and how to get the best health care from the NHS in general and your GP's practice in particular.

Buying a Computer
Buy the system that's right for you, and don't be intimidated by the technical jargon. This guide explains how to make the right decisions, how to keep your information safe, how to get help when you need it, and much more.

Safe as Houses
Don't become a crime statistic! Check out the security of your home using this book and you'll be able to tip the odds against the burglar.

Buying a Second-hand Car
Avoid the common mistakes people make when buying used cars by following the advice from the *Which?* experts.

Countdown to Moving House
Buying and selling property, and moving itself, are stressful activities. Stay in control and leave nothing to chance by using this book's tips and checklists.

Here's just a flavour of some of the reports planned for future issues of *Which?*

- Multimedia PCs on test • Tumble driers • Stereo systems
- Compact cameras • Current accounts • Claiming on car insurance
- Health insurance • Shopping on the Internet • Washing machines
- Large family cars • Postal deliveries • Council Tax
- Package holidays • Credit reference agencies • Best Buy PEPs

So why not take up our trial offer today?

▼ SUMMARY OF OFFER

3 free issues of Which? as they are published • Just fill in the delayed direct debiting instruction below and post it to Which?, FREEPOST, Hertford X, SG14 1YB • If you do not wish to continue beyond the free trial period simply write to us at the address above, and to your Bank/Building Society to cancel your direct debiting instruction, before the 1st payment is due • Your first payment will be due on the 1st of the month 3 months after the date you sign the mandate (so for example, if you sign the mandate on 15th August, your 1st payment is due on 1st November) • No action is necessary if you wish to continue after the free trial. We will send you Which? each month for the current price of £14.75 a quarter, until you cancel or until we advise you of a change in price • We would give you at least 6 weeks notice in advance of any change in price, so you would have plenty of time to decide whether to continue – you are of course free to cancel at any time.

Offer subject to acceptance. Which? Ltd, Reg in England Reg No 677665. Reg Office 2 Marylebone Road, London NW1 4DF. Reg under the Data Protection Act. As result of responding to this offer, your name and address might be added to a mailing list. This could be used by ourselves (Which? Ltd, or our parent company Consumers' Association) or other companies for sending you offers in the future. If you prefer not to receive such offers, please write to Dept DNP3 at the above Hertford address or tick the box on the coupon if you only want to stop offers from other companies. You will not be sent any future offers for 5 years, in compliance with the British Code of Advertising and Sales Promotion.

- - - - - - - - - - - **▼ DETACH HERE ▼** - - - - - - - - - - -

Your name and address in BLOCK CAPITALS PLEASE

Name (Mr/Mrs/Miss/Ms)   Address

                                                    Postcode

To: Which?, FREEPOST, Hertford X, SG14 1YB
Please send me the next 3 months' issues of Which? magazine as they appear. I understand that I am under no obligation – if I do not wish to continue after the 3 months' free trial, I can cancel my order before my first payment is due on the 1st of the month 3 months after the date I sign the mandate. But if I decide to continue I need do nothing – my subscription will bring me monthly Which? for the current price of £14.75 a quarter.

Direct Debiting Instruction Please pay Which? Ltd Direct Debits from the account detailed on this Instruction subject to the safeguards assured by The Direct Debit Guarantee. I understand that this Instruction may remain with Which? and if so, details will be passed electronically to any bank or building society.

Signed   Date

Bank/Building Society account in the name of   Name and address of your Bank/Building Society in BLOCK CAPITALS PLEASE

To:

*Banks/Building Societies may decline to accept Direct Debits to certain types of account other than current accounts

*Bank/Building Society Acct. No.

Tick here if you do not wish to receive promotional mailings from other companies ☐

Bank/Building Society Sort Code

                                                    Postcode

- - - - - **NO STAMP NEEDED • SEND NO MONEY** - - - - -